CONTENTS

Everything you need to know about Fortnite in once place! With this guide by your side, the **Victory Royale awaits!**

2 BATTLE BASICS

We reveal the winning tactics used by all the best Fortnite players! If you want to get ahead of your opponents, the answer is in here!

10 BOOSTING XP QUICKLY

The inside tricks and tips that can help you get maximum XP for minimum effort. Step this way to that 100 ranking...

12 DROP IT LIKE IT'S HOT

Getting off to a good start is essential to being a great Fortnite player. We'll show you how you can give yourself an advantage from the moment your boots land on the island!

14 GUIDE TO STEALTH

Shh! If they don't know you're coming, how can they stop you? Our sneaky guide to success reveals all...

20 THE ULTIMATE GUIDE TO SNIPING

Master Fortnite's trickiest skill – sniping! Everything from where to snipe from, what to look out for, and how to make sure you take out opponents first time, every time.

22 BUILDING GUIDE

Being a master builder can make all the difference, especially in the later stages of a Battle Royale. Good job we show you how it's done then!

26 ELIMINATIONS ON THE MOVE!

Master the full range of vehicles available in Fortnite. Take out your opponents and be gone before they've even realised the danger!

32 SICK SKINS

Fortnite is all about looking good, so here are some of our favourite skins – there's something for every budget in here!

42 50 THINGS TO TRY IN FORTNITE

So you think you know Fortnite, huh? Our list of challenges and hidden extras will make you an even better Fortnite player, and breathe new life into your gaming!

WATCH YOUR PENNIES!

Although there are lots of cool things to spend V-Bucks on in Fortnite, there is nothing you can buy that gives you an advantage, so you don't NEED to spend money. If you do want to blow some V-Bucks on a Battle Pass or some cool extras, always make sure to check with an adult before you go crazy with their credit card!

Little Brother

Published 2021.
Little Brother Books, Ground Floor, 23 Southernhay East, Exeter, Devon, EX1 1QL
Printed in Turkey.
books@littlebrotherbooks.co.uk | www.littlebrotherbooks.co.uk

BATTLE BASICS

If you're going to come out on top and **rack up some Victory Royales**, then you'll need to have **mastered** some of these **battle basics**! Read on for **all the information** you need to come out on top!

UPGRADE YOUR WEAPONS →

The weapons in the game are colour coded as well as star rated, so keep an eye out for any opportunity to dump an existing weapon in favour of a more powerful version of the same gun. You'll do more damage that way. Don't forget that you can use upgrade benches to improve the weapons you already have too!

PACK FOR ALL OCCASIONS ↓

Try to make sure you make full use of your inventory. Don't carry lots of the same weapon – try to make sure you at least have a short-range weapon like a shotgun and a mid-range weapon such as an assault rifle. You should also try and carry a Shield Potion or MedKit in case you sustain damage, and a sniper rifle for long distance combat.

PLAY SMART ↓

The aim of the game is to be the last player standing, not to get the most kills. That means you will do better if you play smart. Don't take potshots at enemies a long way off, drawing attention to your position – you should only be firing your weapons when you've got the drop on them and can be sure you'll be able to eliminate them!

SEE WHAT YOU HEAR ↑

In the settings, you'll find an option to visualise sound effects. Do it! With this setting enabled, you'll see on-screen hints about which directions footsteps, gunfire and other noises are coming from. It can make all the difference in knowing when you're about to find yourself in danger – to be forewarned is to be forearmed!

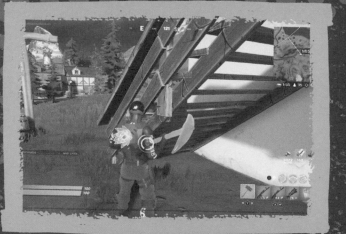

STEADY YOURSELF

It's almost impossible to hit anyone from distance while you're moving. Your accuracy will be considerably increased by crouching and looking down the sights of your weapon. After taking a couple of shots, get up and move before you are damaged by return fire, then repeat the process until your opponent is eliminated!

HIT THE WEAK SPOT

When harvesting or attacking a structure with your harvesting tool, always aim for the weak spot – it appears as a circle when you start swinging. Hitting it will cause the item you are attacking to be harvested quicker, meaning it will disappear with fewer hits and minimising the noise you have to make as a result.

ARRANGE YOUR GOODIES

Put your weapons next to each other in your inventory so that you can switch between them quickly in combat. Having to cycle past a MedKit or Shield Potion to find your next weapon will cost you valuable split seconds that could make all the difference between defeat and victory!

WOODEN IT BE LOVELY

It's tempting to use metal when building defensive structures when you come under fire, but don't be tempted! Stick to wood. Metal becomes stronger than wood after a few seconds, but wood is actually sturdier when it first spawns so will do a better job of protecting you if you're being attacked!

WERE YOU BORN IN A BARN?

Try to avoid giving your opponents any clues about where you are. When you enter or leave a building, shut the door behind you so no-one knows you've been in, and try to walk while crouching rather than sprinting as you make much less noise that way.

IT'S A TRAP! →

Don't forget to use traps! There are lots of different sorts, but they can be put to great use. They're very visible out in the open, so are best used inside buildings. The ideal location is right inside a doorway, in a room with a Loot Chest. Lay your trap and close the door, then head on out of there. Anyone passing who opens the door in search of the Loot Chest is in for a shock. It's always nice to get an elimination from a trap you laid five minutes earlier miles away from your current location too!

HARVEST FESTIVAL ↑

Harvest materials whenever you can safely do so, especially at the start of the game (where the odds are that you'll have more time and space to do so). As well as upgrading weapons, the materials you accumulate can be used for building structures later in the game.

DON'T THROW UP! ↓

When you are using grenades, never use them to attack someone at the top of a hill, mountain or cliff if you are at the bottom. Gravity is NOT your friend here, and it's all too easy for your explosive missile to land right back where it started – blowing you to pieces in the process!

ZIG WHEN THEY ZAG ↓

When crossing open spaces, you're a sitting duck. Make life hard for anyone thinking of taking a potshot at you by moving in a zig zag pattern (but change direction randomly so it's hard for them to predict) and jumping up and down occasionally. This makes you much harder to hit while you are in an otherwise vulnerable situation.

WATCH YOUR RESOURCES ↑

It's easy to lose track of your building resources during a game, especially if you've had to throw a few structures up in combat. Keep an eye on how much you have of each material and if you need to spend a bit of time restocking, then make sure you do it so you aren't caught short when it really matters!

THE QUICK-SWITCH RELOAD ⬆

If you run out of ammo during a fight, it's often quicker to change to the next weapon in your inventory than to reload – you'll be able to fire straight away without having to wait, and those few seconds can make all the difference.

ALL ABOUT THAT BASE ⬆

If you're attacking a structure built by one of your opponents, concentrate on the base. Destroy the bottom and the whole structure will topple – often causing them some serious damage in the process. Of course, if the building has a wide base then this technique won't work too well, but if they have built a tall sniping tower, it can be a very effective solution.

I CAN SEE YOU! ⬇

Use the third person perspective that Fortnite employs to your advantage. By crouching behind cover, you can still see where your opponents are, making it easier for you to pop out and take the perfect shot.

DON'T CHOP DOWN FORESTS! ⬇

When harvesting wood, don't completely destroy the trees you are gathering wood from. Instead, leave them with one or two hits left. Opponents may spot a tree disappearing from a distance, which gives your position away. Leaving it standing is more discreet, and it doesn't deprive you of potential cover either!

THROW IT AWAY ⬅

If you find items you don't want to take with you, then try to make sure the next player to come along can't benefit from them either. If you're near a cliff edge, try throwing weapons, Shield Potions and MedKits somewhere inaccessible or back into the storm, and throw grenades so that they explode and can't be picked up by anyone else (without drawing attention to your position of course). If you can't carry Bandages or small Shield Potions but can drink them for even 1HP then do it! Be selfish, basically – don't hand any potential advantages to your opponents!

AVOID ZIPLINES →

You might think it's cool to use ziplines to move around the map high above your opponents' heads, but it really isn't the best way to travel. It's hard to shoot accurately while moving, and you're a sitting duck for anyone looking to pick you off because you're moving in a straight line (obviously). Throw in the fact that they make a noise as well as making it easy for opponents to ambush you at the end of a zipline, it's a pretty clear NO!

USE CAMPFIRES TO HEAL ↓

As well as Bandages and MedKits, you can use campfires to heal. Simply light them when you find one and stay by it – your health will increase back towards 100%. If you have wood, you can stoke the fire to recover more quickly but be careful as the smoke can give your location away to nearby players!

BUILD TO SURVIVE ↑

If you need to heal and there's no cover nearby, make sure you build a simple structure to provide cover while you're vulnerable. Just a square room with four walls and a roof will keep you safe long enough to get your health or shield back to where it needs to be!

I'M UP HERE! →

In any fight, the player with the higher ground will have the advantage. Whenever you can try and stay high – near the top of cliffs or mountains – instead of running down into valleys. Don't stand right on the top of a ridge, however, as that leaves you visible to opponents on either side of the ridge, silhouetted nicely against the sky. Instead, stay high but drop down slightly onto one side so that you are less visible but still have the high ground advantage.

AIM FOR THE BODY ⬇

Headshots may look awesome, but it's a smaller target. If you're in a situation where you can fire a couple of shots quickly – especially when you are at close quarters – aim for the torso as it is a bigger target and you are less likely to miss!

RIGHT WEAPON, RIGHT TIME ⬆

Make sure you're carrying the right weapon for the situation you are in. If you enter a house where you know any combat will be at close quarters, switch to a shotgun or machine gun first so you aren't caught by surprise. Similarly, if you're crossing a large open space, there's little point in having your shotgun equipped because any combat is likely to be at distance.

FISHING FOR COMPLIMENTS ⬇

Fishing in the waters round the island can be a great way to get new weapons. You need to be sure you are along, and try to fish from within cover (such as a bush) if possible. You won't just catch fish – it's not unusual to pull a weapon or two out of the water too. The different types of fish can repair your health or armour, while some have other special powers too – get to know them all and make the most of any opportunities you get to fish!

DEMOLITION DERBY ⬆

If you're inside a structure, the best way to harvest materials is to focus on the internal walls and floors. By leaving the outside walls alone, you won't be destroying your own cover – meaning you can get on with stockpiling without worrying about someone picking you off from a distance!

KEEP THAT MAGAZINE FULL ➡

Don't forget that your weapons only hold a certain number of shots each, and that you'll need to reload. Get into the habit of reloading after every single battle you have – there's nothing more annoying than forgetting and then running out of ammo after a couple of shots against the next opponent you encounter.

HARPOON GUN →

The Harpoon Gun can help you fish more quickly, minimising the risk to you from being otherwise engaged, but it can also be very useful for grabbing items and bringing them near to you. If you don't want to risk being shot at while picking up loot, use a harpoon gun to bring the loot to you! You can do the same trick to opponents too – just make sure you are quick to switch to a shotgun once they are up close and personal!

FORAGED GOODS ↓

Keep an eye out on the floor as you make your way round the map. There are often foraged goods that you can eat to give a small boost to your shield or health. It might not look like much, but it all adds up and you never know – it might make all the difference!

QUICK BUILD ↑

Get into the habit of building walls as soon as you come under fire. By putting something solid between you and the person shooting at you, you can buy yourself some valuable seconds to pinpoint their location and form a plan of attack.

USE COVER ↓

There are lots of bushes around the island, so make sure you use them when you can. The cover they provide makes you harder for opponents to spot and can make all the difference in giving you a vital headstart in a battle! Similarly, if you come under fire, leaping into nearby bushes can buy you vital seconds to recover and regroup.

BE MINDFUL OF YOUR SURROUNDINGS ↑

Don't get so focused on one opponent or destination that you forget that there are 100 players in a Battle Royale! You should be constantly looking all around you to check for nearby movement, to avoid anyone sneaking up behind you!

RAMP IT UP ←

If you have time, a ramp can be a big help in a firefight. As you run towards your opponent build a couple of ramps and run up them, firing down on them as you jump from the top. It's likely the ramp will absorb a couple of shots from them, giving you a much-needed advantage and hopefully eliminating them before they can eliminate you!

SHARE THE WEALTH! →

If you're playing as part of a group, make sure you share what you find in Loot Chests and around the map. There's no point in three of you having an inventory of pure awesome if your fourth player only has a common pistol to survive with. They'll end up being eliminated quickly and making life harder for you all, so make sure you share equally when you're playing as part of a group!

CAUGHT IN A TRAP ←

A great way to rack up eliminations is lootbaiting – that is, concealing yourself near a chest, supply drop, llama or a vanquished opponent's dropped armoury and waiting. When an over-excited player rushes in to pick up the goodies – BOOM, you will be ready and waiting with the element of surprise!

BUILD TO CLIMB →

Don't forget that you can build ramps to quickly ascend to parts of the map that might take you a while to reach otherwise – especially up steep cliffs or mountainsides. In particular, this technique can be very handy when trying to outrun the storm, when it's easy to forget that you can build up to climb mountains instead of having to move sideways to find a footpath that you can run up!

SEAL IN THE REBOOT VAN ←

If you're playing duos, trios or squads then you might find yourself in a situation where you need to reboot a team mate at the Reboot Van. The problem? You're a sitting duck while you do it. To solve that issue, make sure you build around it – ideally using metal so it takes longer for enemies to break it down!

STOP YOUR OPPONENTS REACHING THE REBOOT VAN →

If you eliminate an opponent in multiplayer but they still have team mates in the game, they may grab the Reboot Card to save their fallen comrade. Don't make it easy for them. Firstly, you can build over and around the area where you eliminated the player, making it harder for their team mates to get the Reboot Card. Secondly, you can also build around the nearest Reboot Van itself, making it more difficult for opposing players to reach it. The extra time it will take them to destroy your building work can buy you enough time to launch an assault on them!

BOOSTING XP QUICKLY

Increasing your XP means a **higher tier** in the game and, if you have the Battle Pass, **more goodies unlocked!** Here are some great ways to get XP quickly – giving you access to more goodies into the bargain.

WAIT FOR SUPERCHARGE DAYS

Sometimes, you'll see that your XP bar is flashing yellow and it reads 'XP supercharged'. When that's the case (and there's not always any particular pattern to when it happens), you'll get double XP points. That makes it a great time to finish off any achievements you are close to completing. In fact, it's often wise to leave challenges ALMOST complete until a supercharged day, and then finish them off to make the most of the extra XP points!

BUY IT

It's not the most glorious way of advancing your status in the game, but you can always buy extra tiers as part of the battle pass, or separately further into the game. It will cost you money, but if you're running out of time to reach tier 100 and unlock all that goodness, then forking out for some extra tiers makes sense.

CHALLENGE YOURSELF

Read all the various challenges available to you before each match and try to focus on them. You can often pick up lots of XP for simple things, like visiting a particular location or upgrading a weapon. Always know what you need to do to get easy points, and focus on that!

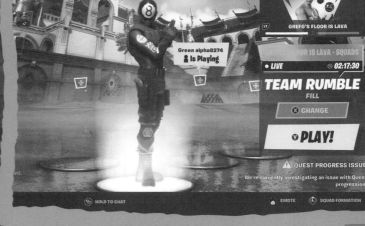

LAST MAN STANDING

Good performances tend to bring in lots of XP points, so make sure you're lasting long into games in order to improve your performance. It helps that the longer you stay in the game, the more things you can do so you get a double whammy by making it into the top 10 consistently.

GET READY TO RUMBLE!

Sometimes, completing challenges in Battle Royale can be difficult as, you know, there are other players trying to eliminate you. Playing Team Rumble means that you'll respawn whenever you are shot, so it can be a much more efficient way to increase your XP. However, don't be a selfish player – you'll annoy your team mates if you ignore the game and just focus on challenges, so make sure you get the balance right!

XP COINS

Dotted around the map you'll find different types of XP coins. They'll all give you a quick and easy XP boost so make sure you grab them when you see them! Be careful though – make sure its safe to get them first so that you don't get eliminated on your way to picking up the coin!

TEAM ASSIST

When you are playing in duos, trios or squads, lots of challenges can be completed when other members of your party do them. You'll all contribute to each other's totals, so by working together you can get more done! For example, if you have a challenge to open a certain number of Ammo Boxes or Loot Chests, then those opened by your squad mates will contribute towards your total. Nice!

DROP IT LIKE IT'S HOT

Getting off to a **great start** is so important in Fortnite, so it's worth spending a little time practicing your landing. Landing where you want to go and before anyone else gets there means you can **grab the best** loot first and play the game on the front foot.

JUDGE YOUR DISTANCE

If you've dropped a marker, then you'll get a distance reading showing you how far you are from it. The ideal distance to jump from the battle bus is around 1,200m away from your marker. When you leave the Battle Bus, dive straight down at the shallowest angle possible, with your marker in front of you. Your glider will open automatically, and you'll know you've timed things right if it opens with around 400m to your target.

PLAN YOUR STARTING POINT

It's important to decide where you want to land early – the Battle Bus' path is visible while you wait for the game to fill up. It pays to study it before the game starts and drop a marker so that you'll be able to judge your distance when things get going.

PRACTICE MAKES PERFECT

With each new season, the odds are you'll find particular places that you prefer to start from. Explore the whole map and try and have one preferred landing site in each quarter of the map, so that you'll always have options. If you keep rotating between these sites, you'll start to get a feel for when to jump from the Battle Bus and when you are on for a good landing and when things have gone wrong. The more you practice specific locations, the better you'll get.

GRAB EVERYTHING YOU CAN SEE

Pick up every weapon you see from the moment you land until your inventory is full and you need to swap items out. It makes no sense to leave a weapon behind only for someone who landed five seconds after you did to pick it up and eliminate you with it! While you have space, make sure you pick everything up as you pass it.

TAKE IN THE VIEWS

As you're coming in to land, make sure you spin a quick 360º to see if there are any other players behind you heading for the same spot. Be sure to look up and down too, as they may be above you!

LAND ON A ROOF

It's often best to land on the roof of a building and use your harvesting tool to break through and then work your way down from the top floor. As long as you've made sure no-one followed you through the gap you made, anyone you encounter in the building you've entered will be in front of you – and you'll have the higher ground too.

HAVE A BACK-UP PLAN

If the place you are heading for looks too busy for your liking, then it's a good idea to have an alternative landing spot nearby already lined up. If you've followed our advice to consistently land in the same four locations, you'll soon find a suitable secondary landing site near to each one, if things are looking a bit too hot to handle at your first choice!

GET OUT OF DODGE

If you realise too late that the landing spot you've chosen is hotter than Hades itself, look for a vehicle in the last few metres of your descent. If you get your timing right, you can land on top of one, get straight into it, and hightail it out of there to somewhere a bit more peaceful!

LANDING QUICKLY

If you want to be on the ground before anyone else, jump out of the Battle Bus immediately, while you are still over the sea. Head straight down and the chute will open based on sea level, meaning you can glide to land and be on the deck before anyone else! It doesn't mean you'll find the best weapons though...

GUIDE TO STEALTH

Now, there are **loads of different ways** to play Fortnite – that's the really cool thing about it. What you wear, where you drop, which weapons you favour – there really is **something for everyone**. In this section, we talk you through the best ways to play Fortnite in a stealthy way, making yourself a **hard target** to find and hopefully conserving your health until there are only a **few rivals standing!**

DRESS SMART Playing in a stealthy way starts even before you get to Spawn Island. The first rule of stealth is to blend into your surroundings – if you stick out like a sore thumb, then your opponents will see you from the other side of the island! Think carefully about the skin you select, and choose something that will be hard to spot. Skins like Rippley or Peely are brightly coloured and can be seen from miles away. Choose something black or dark green to blend into shadows and backgrounds – our favourite is the Plastic Patroller skin, but there are plenty that will do the job!

ACCESSORISE CAREFULLY It's not just about the skin you select when it comes to being hard to spot. There's no point in wearing a camo skin top to toe, then throwing in a dayglo rucksack. Look at every part of your outfit to make sure it isn't going to attract unwanted attention. Don't bother with back bling at all, make sure weapon wraps are off (or set to something dark), and don't use a chem trail to make it harder for other players to spot you as you enter the game. Even a dark glider can be helpful. Take it all into consideration!

DON'T GET INVOLVED

Remember that the aim of Fortnite is to be the last player standing – not to rack up the most eliminations. If you want to increase your chances of making it into the last few rounds of combat, the answer is not to get involved with combat unless you are extremely close and have the element of surprise. Firing at opponents that you might not be able to eliminate immediately will only draw attention to your position – the opposite of what you want when playing stealthily.

KEEP IT QUIET
As you pick up weapons in the game, prioritise those that are silenced. These make it harder for other gamers to pinpoint your position, though there is a tradeoff in how much damage they can do – especially at distance. However, if you're playing stealthily, you shouldn't really engage any opponents unless they are quite close, so this is less of an issue.

EXPLOSIVES CAN BE STEALTHY

Just because you don't want to draw attention to yourself doesn't mean you can't make a noise every now and then! Explosives weapons such as grenades or mines are perfect for a stealth game because you don't make a sound when you thrown them or plant them – by the time they go boom, you should be nowhere near them! Grenades can be especially useful when thrown at enemies from cover.

HAVE A BACK-UP WEAPON IN YOUR LOCKER

Although you shouldn't actively look to fire at opponents who are a distance away, there's always the risk of someone spotting you and firing on you with an Automatic Rifle or similar. If all you have are silenced handguns and submachine guns, you'll struggle to hit them at a distance so it's often worth carrying an Assault Rifle yourself for such an emergency – just make sure it's a back-up plan and not your go-to weapon!

SNIPERS BEWARE

The sniper rifle is extremely noisy and will betray your location to anyone nearby, but it can still be a useful ally in a stealthy game as long as you are competent using it. The key is to always use it from within cover, and to always move position immediately after using it so that no-one can sneak up on your position based on the sound of the gunfire.

WHERE TO DROP

Getting off to a good start is key to a solid stealth game. You need to avoid hot drops, so look for somewhere a good distance away from the Battle Bus' initial flight path. Named locations are a big risk – instead try to focus on smaller locations near woodland or good hiding places.

HIDE AND SEEK!

There are lots of places around the map that you can jump into to hide from opponents, and it's amazing how few players actually take advantage of these, or investigate them in case someone is hiding in them. Dumpsters and portaloos can be a great place to hole up should you find yourself in need of somewhere to lay low for a while.

BACKED INTO A CORNER

If you are a happy camper and comfortable waiting in a building for opponents to blunder in, then make sure you put yourself in a corner so that you can't be surprised. Make sure you aren't by a window, or that there isn't a walkway above your head as these mean you can be spotted by opponents without you knowing you're in their sights. Ideally, look for a corner of the room that's in shadow, and make sure you can see all doorways into the room so you can respond if anyone enters.

BUSHCAMPING!

It might not be the most popular tactic, but the many bushes around the island make ideal cover for anyone looking to keep a low profile. Position yourself near the edge of the bush and look down the sights of your weapon and you'll be able to see out of the bush perfectly – but no-one will be able to see you!

WALK DO NOT RUN!

When you sprint in Fortnite, your opponents will be able to hear you. Crouch down, however, and you'll move much more slowly and – crucially – quietly. If you're hoping to avoid detection then it's absolutely essential that you spend most (if not all) of the game in a crouched stance. It's especially important when you are in buildings, as your footsteps will make it easier for others to find you.

I WOULD WALK 500 MILES
Although it's tempting to jump into a vehicle, the fact is they are incredibly noisy and they announce your arrival long before opponents can see you. Even if you leap out of the vehicle when you reach your destination, anyone nearby will know you are in the area and may well start looking for you. As such, leave vehicles unless you are caught in the storm and desperate to escape!

BACK TO THE STORM

Another great piece of advice if you want to play stealthily is to try and position yourself in a covered location (inside a building or hidden in a bush) near the edge of the storm circle at each phase of play. That way, once you know that no-one is going to burst out of the storm behind you, you can focus on what's ahead of you. As a rule, the closer you are to the middle of the circle, the more action there will be, so hanging around on the outside is a smart idea.

TREETOPS
A nifty way to stay out of sight is to build a ramp up to the top of a tree and hide there. Don't forget to destroy your ramp though, otherwise it's a bit of a giveaway! You'll be amazed how many players don't look up, so you can stay out of the way on your treetop – or use the element of surprise to drop down behind someone and eliminate them!

DON'T LEAVE IT LATE
A very useful piece of advice is to move steadily towards the new storm circle in each phase (assuming you aren't already in it). Don't immediately run hell for leather for it, as you might get picked off, but leaving it to the last minute can also leave you a sitting duck as you run towards it. By starting to move for it in a measured way, you can plan your route so that you avoid having to cross vast expanses of open ground, for example, giving yourself plenty of time to find cover within the storm circle.

THE ULTIMATE GUIDE TO SNIPING

There are **loads of weapons** in Fortnite and they all have their strengths and weaknesses. However, if you master the sniper rifle you can give yourself a **real advantage**, picking off opponents from miles away. Here's all you need to know to become a **sniping expert!**

RELOAD AFTER EVERY SHOT

Although there are a couple of different classes of sniper rifle, you'll need to reload your weapon after every single shot. Don't forget to do this! Sometimes it can be easy to stay zoomed in, looking down the sights and trying to take a second shot. However, there's no point doing so if the only thing you hear when you pull the trigger is a click! After each shot, reload quickly before your next move!

DON'T STAY IN ONE PLACE

Movement is key when using a sniper rifle. It makes a loud noise, so there's a good chance your opponent will figure out roughly where you are, and if there are any opponents nearby, the gunfire will alert them too. It's best to try and move somewhere new after each shot or two if you can, to make it harder for anyone to get a fix on your location.

SHOOT FROM COVER ⬅

Aiming down your sniper scope to get the perfect shot takes a lot of concentration and, because you can't see much going on around you, leaves you vulnerable. You should try to use a sniper rifle from within cover whenever possible. Position yourself near a window in a building, or inside a bush if you're outside.

SNIPER'S NEST ➡

If you need to use your sniper rifle and there isn't any natural cover nearby, consider building a sniping hut. Something simple will suffice; just four walls and a roof can keep you safe. Edit one wall to give yourself a window and you've got a great sniper's hideout.

LEAD YOUR TARGET ⬅

Because you're firing from a long distance away, sniper rifles behave differently to all the other guns in Fortnite. It takes a couple of seconds for your bullet to reach its destination, in which time the person you're aiming at will quite possibly have moved. To counter this, you'll need to 'lead' with your aim, aiming a little way in front of them so that after you fire, the bullet will arrive at the right time to make contact. Aiming directly at them will usually miss, unless your target is standing still.

THINK IN STRAIGHT LINES ➡

Because you need to lead your opponent with your shot, it's often more effective to use a sniper rifle against an opponent who is moving directly towards or away from you. It's easier to predict their path, and if you get it slightly wrong the odds are you'll still hit them even if it's not the headshot you were hoping for. If they are moving left to right, you need to be much more accurate and lead your target more effectively – the slightest mistake and your shot will sail harmlessly past!

HIGH GROUND MATTERS ⬅

Having the high ground makes a huge difference when using a sniper rifle. Aiming down on an opponent makes it easier to hit them – if you are aiming up at your target then they will be a lot harder to hit. When using the sniper rifle, look to get to high ground whenever possible. Alternatively, climb a tower in one of the buildings or build your own (but be careful as the latter option can make it obvious where you are!)

BUILDING GUIDE

There can be no doubt that mastering the building element of Fortnite is what makes the difference between being good at the game and being GREAT at the game. If you want to turn those top ten finishes into awesome Victory Royales, then read on, because we have some master builder tips for you.

QUICK SHIELD

When someone fires on you from a distance, BUILD! This needs to become a built-in reflex because it WILL save you in combat. Throw up two or three walls and use the time to try and see where the shooting is coming from and launch a counter offensive!

RAPUNZEL

Another build to master is the quick tower to gain high ground. Build four walls around you, then jump and build a ramp beneath you. Repeat this process over and over and you can build a tower very quickly indeed, giving yourself the high ground when it comes to combat.

DECOY BUILD

Very often, the sight of a building is enough to provoke an attack from other players as it usually suggests there's someone inside. You can use that to your advantage by building a sniping tower or similar, then taking cover nearby. Opponents entering the area are likely to focus on the deserted building, either by attacking it directly or approaching it with caution. That gives you the ideal opportunity to use the element of surprise to take them out!

STAIRWAY TO HEAVEN

When building staircases, especially up a building, build two staircases (one in front of the other), and climb the back one. The other one will act as a roof, which will do more than keep you dry if it rains. It offers you protection from anyone who tries to pick you off as you climb the stairs!

BUILD AS YOU DROP!

Building ramps to get up mountains is a fairly obvious way that building smartly can help you move around the island, but don't forget you can also build on your way down! If you find yourself with only a sheer drop that's going to either kill you or cost you lots of energy, build platforms extending from the cliff face as you drop down. They'll break your fall so you reach the bottom unscathed. Using this technique can be a great way to escape from seemingly impossible situations!

TAKE THE FIRE ESCAPE

When you're facing an enemy who is inside a building, the odds are they will have the staircases and doorways covered and be expecting you. Instead of doing what they expect you to, why not build up the outside of the building and break your way in through the roof, coming at them from an angle they really won't be expecting?

TRAPPING THE SUPPLY DROP

You can use a building to make it easier to get the supply drop, especially if you're first to the scene. Before the supply drop arrives, build around the landing zone. You can either wait inside the square you've constructed or leave a door in it and hide nearby. The important thing is not to build a roof – yet! Once the supply drop lands, enter the square and edit out the door (if you weren't inside the square to start with) then add a roof. You now have a bit of time and space to open the supply drop and grab the goodies without worrying about being spotted by a sniper!

DIFFERENT MATERIALS

Although wood is the weakest building material available to you, it's the quickest. Brick and metal walls take longer to construct and can be destroyed too easily in the first few seconds so, if you need to build quickly under pressure, always go for wood. Save metal and brick for situations later in the game where you need to build a structure you'll be staying in and will need to survive a serious onslaught!

STOP THE SUPPLY DROP SLIDING

The supply drop often lands on a slop – sometimes on the side of a pretty steep cliff. That means once it's opened, you can spend a lot of time sliding down to catch up with all those lovely goodies, so again – plan ahead. While you are waiting for the supply drop, build a platform for it to land on. By building walls around it, you'll stop the goodies disappearing down the hill, meaning you can grab them quickly and move on!

BUILDING IN TEAMS

If you're playing with team mates, it's usually quite risky if you're all building at the same time. A quick attack can put you at a disadvantage. Instead, try to leave at least one player free, with a weapon equipped and covering the others.

BUILD QUICKLY IN THE FINAL STORM CIRCLE

When there are only a handful of players left, skulking around in the bushes or on the edge of the map really isn't going to cut it. You need to get building and quickly, making sure you add a number of different rooms where you can hide as part of the build. Again though, practice makes perfect and this is something you should practice in creative mode or similar until the different types of structure you can create become almost second nature to you.

AMEND EXISTING BUILDINGS

You don't have to add whole new sections to existing buildings in order to transform them into handy places to hole up. You can destroy an existing solid wall and replace it with a section of brick or metal wall yourself. Edit it to give yourself a window and you now have a great place to hole up while you wait for opponents to wander into range.

ADDING AN EXTENSION

Of course, you don't always have to do all the hard work yourself. Sometimes it makes more sense to simply add to an existing structure – either a building that was already in place on the island, or moving cuckoo-like into a structure vacated by another player (possibly one you have eliminated yourself). It can save you time and give you a great starting point!

DON'T FORGET TO EDIT!

If you've built a structure, don't forget that you can change it too! When you look at one of the walls you've built, you'll be given the chance to edit it – and you can make multiple edits too! That means the solid wall you just built can be edited to feature a handy sniping window. And because you can keep editing it, you can remove the window after taking your shot so that it's harder for your opponent to return fire!

ELIMINATIONS
ON THE MOVE!

There are **plenty of vehicles** available in Fortnite! From time to time, some may be vaulted but there are usually a few different types to use. Here are our **guides to using them**!

GENERAL TIPS

ENGINE NOISES

The first thing you need to know is that vehicles are noisy! If you want to use them, don't be surprised that everyone is going to know your location. You'll be at considerable risk when you exit your vehicle because anyone in the immediate area will know exactly where you are – so be careful!

CHOOSE THE RIGHT WEAPON

If you're getting into a vehicle as a passenger, you can change weapons (and even use MedKits and Shield Potions) while you are on the move, but if you are travelling solo, you need to have both hands on the wheel (no drinking and driving, remember!) That means you'll exit the vehicle in the same state that you entered it. For that reason, you should make sure you have used any health items to max yourself out BEFORE you get in, and you should have a decent weapon equipped to, because that's what you'll be holding when you get out. It's very frustrating to get out of a vehicle to suddenly realise you have 25% health and you're holding a pistol when you have far better options than that available in your inventory!

MOTORBOAT

THE MOTORBOAT IS A REALLY GOOD VEHICLE TO GRAB BECAUSE IT IS FITTED WITH A ROCKET LAUNCHER ON THE FRONT, AND CAN CARRY THE REST OF YOUR SQUAD TOO, FOR EXTRA FIREPOWER!

BOOM!

The rocket launcher on the front of the motorboat can cause plenty of damage but it's a slow moving weapon and it takes time to reload. As such, you'll need to be sure with your first shot and follow up quickly. Take too long, and your target will be returning fire so you need to make those first shots count.

WET WET WET

It won't come as a shock to anyone to know that boats work better in the water – but don't forget that Fortnite's motorboats can operate on land too! They'll sustain damage while they move on the ground, and they aren't especially fast either, but it can be a useful way to take a shortcut between different bodies of water.

WORKING IN A GROUP

You can carry up to three passengers in a motorboat, and they can all fire their weapons too. Working like this as a squad can make them a very attractive proposition – with the rocket launcher on the front and three squad mates laying down covering fire, you can deal a lot of damage using a motorboat!

JUMP ON IN

The biggest weakness of a motorboat, however, is that opponents can jump into the back while you are driving! For that reason, don't get too close to your targets. In particular, resist the temptation to run over anyone you see swimming because if they time it right, they'll be in the boat behind you with a free shot!

GET TO THE CHOPPER!

HELICOPTERS ARE A GOOD CHOICE OF VEHICLE, AS THEY ARE RELATIVELY EASY TO CONTROL AND CAN GET YOU AWAY FROM TROUBLE QUITE EASILY. THEY HAVE NO FITTED WEAPON, SO ARE BEST USED IN A SQUAD IF YOU WANT TO CAUSE DAMAGE – BUT THEY CAN EASILY OUTRUN THE STORM AND THE ABILITY TO FLY OVER MOUNTAINS AND RAVINES IS A DEFINITE ADVANTAGE WHEN ON THE RUN!

THE DECOY CHOPPER

Jumping out of the chopper also works well if you are playing solo. Fly towards an opponent and they will understandably start shooting at the chopper. While they are doing so, jump out (make sure you aren't too high when you do it!) You'll have a couple of seconds to open fire on them while they figure out you've left the chopper and are now shooting at them!

BLADES OF GLORY

If you're in a chopper on your own, you can't fire out of the window – but you can still cause damage to any opponents you spot. By flying low and straight at them, you can cause plenty of damage with the chopper blades – but you'll be very vulnerable to them firing at you, and the chopper won't survive this approach for very long.

SQUAD ELIMINATIONS WITH A CHOPPER

If you're playing as a squad, then a chopper can be a very useful weapon indeed. One of you flies, with the other three taking up positions outside the chopper with their weapons drawn. In this way, you can pick off enemies from the skies. Make sure that you have players on each side of the chopper though, so you have all angles covered.

DROPPING A GRENADE

It can be hard to get direct hits with assault rifles and sniper rifles from a chopper – but it's much easier to stock up with grenades, hover above an opposing squad, and drop as many explosive weapons as you can down on them!

DROPPING IN TO SAY HI

Another great way to take out opponents in a squad is to fly towards your opponents while one or two of you open fire on them. In the chaos, the fourth squad member can jump out of the chopper when it is low enough. The focus of the squad you are attacking will most likely be on the chopper, so the player that jumps out may well find themselves with the element of surprise!

PLANE CRAZY

BE CAREFUL ON YOUR APPROACH!

The planes can be an alluring sight that causes some players to drop their guard and rush for them. That's music to the ears of experienced campers, who will often hide nearby and pick you off as you approach. Be very careful that you don't fall into that trap!

QUICK TURN!

Rolling the plane left or right will mean you can move much quicker than just moving in that direction. If you're under fire, it's absolutely essential that you roll the plan to change direction quickly, otherwise you'll be blasted out of the air in next to no time!

BARREL ROLL

Double tap either shoulder button to perform a barrel roll in that direction. This is another useful tip that will make it much harder for opponents to get a fix on you with a sniper rifle. Think of it as the aeronautical equivalent of zigzagging when crossing an open field on foot!

WHO'S FLYING THIS THING?

If you want to shoot at opponents but are flying solo, you can use the built in gun, but lining up a shot can be hard. Instead, switch to one of the passenger seats (which basically involves wing walking!) and fire off a few shots. Just don't forget that the plane will be losing altitude while you do so, so you need to get back in the cockpit quickly!

SLAM ON THE BRAKES!

One thing you can do in a Fortnite plane that you can't do in a real one is hit the brakes! It's possible, using the air brake, to bring your plane to an almost complete stop. This is a great way to spin quickly in a dogfight so that you can start firing at your opponent's tail!

THIS IS A HIJACKING!

If you're on the ground and a plane is diving to attack you or your structure, you can hijack the plane by jumping and entering it if your timing is good. This will leave you standing on the wing with a clear shot at the pilot, who can do very little about matters! If they are quick, they might move out of the cockpit into another place on the plane, but if you unload into them immediately, they won't have time!

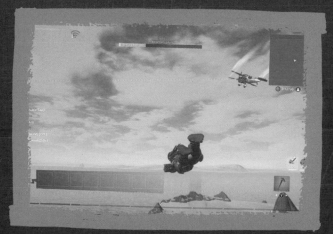

ANYONE CALL AN UBER?

DOTTED AROUND THE MAP YOU'LL FIND LOTS OF DIFFERENT CARS AND TRUCKS. THEY HAVE DIFFERENT STRENGTHS AND WEAKNESSES, BUT HERE'S A GUIDE TO GETTING THE MOST OUT OF THEM!

DRIVE-BY

If you're driving a car, you can't fire out of the windows if you're alone. If you are playing in a duo, trio or squad, however, your buddies can smash the windows and lay some fire down! Check that the car you are selecting can carry you all though – some are only two seaters so there isn't always room for everyone!

MOW 'EM DOWN!

You can cause lots of damage to opponents by hitting them at speed in a car, but it's not always easy to do! If you want to rack up some kills using this technique, then you'll want to get behind the wheel of a sports car or similar – you're looking for something fast with good handling to make it easier to line those opponents up and drive straight over them!

HORSES FOR COURSES

Sports cars may have plenty of speed, but they are pretty useless once they leave the tarmac. If you are looking to head cross-country, then you are much better off in a truck or a lorry cab as these behemoths just keep on going over all kinds of terrain.

THAT'LL BUFF OUT

Like all vehicles in the game, cars and trucks take damage as they are fired on, and if they hit anything while driving. Keep an eye on your damage metre and bail out if it's getting low. You should also check the damage level of any car you find to make sure it's not in a bad way to start with. When cars are badly damaged they tend to start blowing smoke or even burst into flames – if that happens, leave well alone!

IT'S NOT A SHIELD

Don't fall into the trap of thinking the car's damage metre is like an extra shield – it isn't. You can still take direct hits from any bullets that hit you through the window, or while you are leaning out firing (if you're a passenger). And if the car is hit with anything explosive, like a rocket launcher or a grenade, then you'll be toast either way!

GET CLEAR

You can't hurt team-mates if you're in a car, so don't worry about ploughing into them during a firefight. In fact, you can use it to your advantage – if you are in a car and you have a team-mate in trouble, driving into them at speed will send them flying to safety!

CRAZY FUEL

Don't forget that cars need fuel, so keep an eye on how much you have! There's nothing worse than running out whilst in the middle of combat, leaving yourself a sitting duck, so be sure to check how much fuel a car has before you decide whether to take it or not – there may be another one nearby with a full tank!

FILL HER UP

If you're planning on using a car as a big part of your Fortnite strategy, then you should make sure you (or someone in your squad if playing multiplayer) is carrying at least one can of petrol to get you between petrol stations. It goes without saying that you should always fill up to the max when you are at a petrol station too!

SICK SKINS

One sure way to stand out in Fortnite is through your choice of skin. It's only cosmetic though – there's no particular gaming advantage to be had by spending your hard-earned V-Bucks on looking cool. However, if you do want to splash a little cash on upgrading the way you look in-game, here are some of our favourite skins. We've split them into the different categories available so that you can find something to fit your budget nice and quickly!

UNCOMMON SKINS

WHIPLASH

Looking ready to roll in her yellow biking leathers, Whiplash is one seriously cool looking lady. It's a shame there are no motorbikes on the island for her to make the most of, but you'll have plenty of fun using the vehicles that are available!

MATCHPOINT

Looking cool as a cucumber in her tennis whites, Match Point is here to cause a very different kind of racket! Her pale outfit means she'll blend into a snowy background with ease, and she looks pretty ace too. Ace! Geddit?

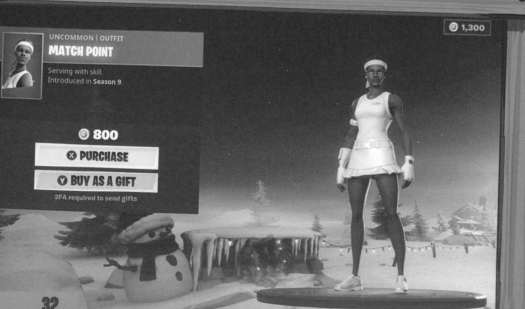

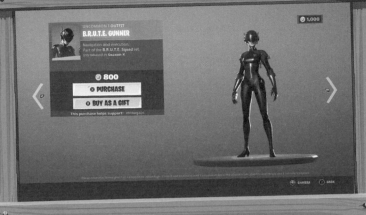

B.R.U.T.E. GUNNER

Is there anything cooler than an all-black outfit? Nope, we didn't think so. The tight fit of this leather and latex number suits her look perfectly, and has the added bonus of being hard to spot when lurking in the shadows too!

MASKED MARAUDER

One of our favourite aspects of the Masked Marauder skin is that you can customise it by changing the colour and design of your banner – which will then show on her T-shirt. How awesome is that? It adds longevity to what is already a great skin!

CHILL COUNT

Brrr! Bit nippy out, isn't it? Well, you won't be feeling the cold if you're using the Chill Count skin. Part of the Permafrost set from the start of Chapter 2, it comes complete with a hood for extra warmth.

SCARLET DEFENDER

With selectable styles that enable further customisation, Scarlett Defender is one of Fortnite's older skins, debuting way back in Season 3. That doesn't make it any less cooler, with that bold flash of colour and matching gloves and accessories making for an awesome look.

RARE SKINS

DREAM

Like something you aren't sure if you really saw, there's an ethereal quality to the Dream skin. The dark purple colours look awesome, especially when combined with the glowing motif on the vest – but be warned, it makes you more visible at night!

BUBBLE BOMBER

Quiet, subtle and understated. None of those words can be used to describe this franky ridiculous and over the top outfit. Bright pink with funky hair, this candy commando may look sweet, but she packs a powerful punch!

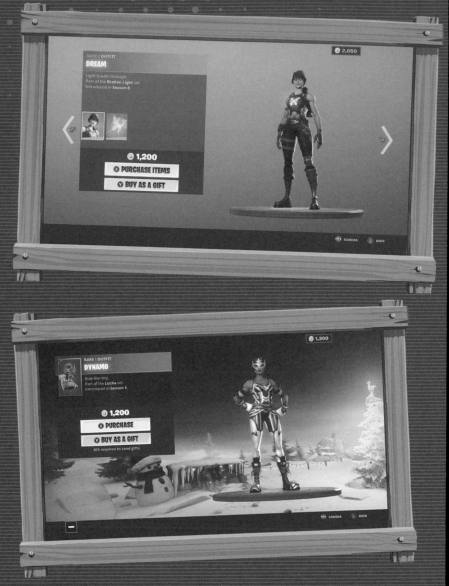

DYNAMO

Nope, not the Yorkshire magician (though he would make a pretty cool skin, come to think of it...) Dynamo instead channels the spirit of crazy Mexican wrestlers, with her lycra outfit and facemask! Not a woman to be messed with!

RUCKUS

One of the Wasteland Warriors from all the way back in Season 6, Ruckus joins us from a Mad Max-inspired world where, despite having to scavenge an outfit from whatever he can find, he still manages to look both cool and terrifying at the same time. Some guys have all the luck...

SPARKPLUG

You'd think that with some vehicles in Fortnite being clamped, a mechanic-themed skin would have a few tricks up her sleeve to get the cars usable again, but sadly that's not the case. Instead, you can use the Sparkplug skin to hang out at gas stations, waiting for your opponents to come to you...

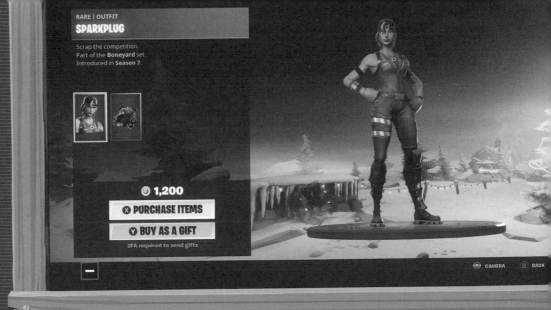

ARCTICA

Another outfit inspired by the frozen wastelands of the Fortnite island, Arctica looks like she is wrapped in tinfoil. In fact, the last thing you might see is your own reflection in her outfit as she scales down a snowy cliff face to take you by surprise!

COZY CHOMPS

We're going to need a bigger boat. Actually, that's nonsense. Cozy Chomps is perhaps the least realistic-looking shark outfit we've ever seen. That said, there's still plenty of fun to be had in confusing opponents when swimming. While they figure out whether to shoot you or catch you with a rod, you can make your escape!

MAYHEM

Another Wasteland Warrior, Mayhem was ahead of the game when it came to wearing a facemask, as you can see. Selectable styles mean you can add a few personal touches to the look too – what's not to love about that?

EPIC SKINS

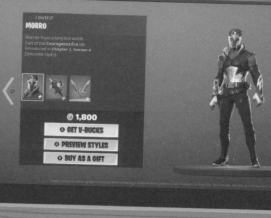

MORRO

This guy is a warrior from a long-lost world but his bright outfit makes him look more like a superhero wannabe to us. His bright colours are bold and dashing, so he sticks out like a sore thumb. Perhaps the reason why his warrior world is long lost...

BRITE GUNNER

There's a lot to unpack here.
The fearsome glint in the eye.
The armour protecting his sword arm and his leading leg in combat.
The cuddly teddy and rainbow picture on his shirt. Wait, what? Some people are just full of contradictions we suppose.

CHAOS AGENT

This skin looks well-quipped to explore the island's watery depths, but the rubber outfit look may not be to everyone's taste. However, he's very hard to spot when lurking in the shadows.

SNAKE EYES

Not sure how this fella came to be called Snake Eyes because, well, you can't see his eyes. In fact, this highly classified ninja master gives pretty much nothing away – but his katana makes for awesome back bling and an excellent harvesting tool.

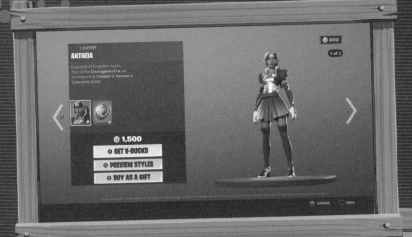

ANTHEIA

She's a friend of Morro's, and her outfit choices are no less understated. There's definitely a Wonder Woman vibe to her garb, and the cute blue bow on the front of her dress suggests she's a harmless little thing. Don't be fooled.

BEEF BOSS

The Durrr Burger franchise would certainly fail even the most cursory inspection from the local Health & Safety team, but that doesn't make this outfit any less desirable. Forget the clown, this is the most desirable burger mascot of all time – and now he can be yours!

CASTOR

Initially found wandering through Wailing Woods, this Merlin lookalike is an old-school warlock. Except for the fact that he is a dab hand with automatic assault rifles and rocket launchers. That bit's definitely not old school.

SANCTUM

Someone's been watching a bit too much Batman, don't you think? Exuding a Bane vibe to the max, this ghostly vampire apparition is not the kind of fellow you want to run into on a dark night. Deliciously scary.

LEGENDARY SKINS

ICE QUEEN
She looks like she's just jumped off a sledge and is about to offer you some Turkish Delight. This cold-hearted killer was first spotted way back in Season 7 and is most at home on the snowy mountains.

JOHN WICK
It's impossible to combine a list of the best skins in Fortnite without mentioning the John Wick skin. One of the game's first nods to including contemporary culture from outside the game as part of the game, this skin is still one of the most loved and wanted in the game.

DJ BOP
This superstar DJ has got the lot. Crazy llama looks, an outfit with flashing lights, and the ability to bring the beat to wherever the party is. Will you be able to hear the music over the gunfire though?

MOISTY MERMAN
In movies, getting special effects just right can make all the difference. This half man, half fish creature has done things backwards, having the head of a fish and the body of a human. Doesn't he know it's meant to be the other way round?

WUKONG

This beast from the Far East is not in the mood to take any prisoners. An oriental master of disaster, his rippling muscles are ready to lift whatever weapons he can get his hands on, and we would not want to be in the way once this guy is armed to the teeth!

OMEN

There's something incredibly chilling about the simplicity of this outfit, especially when taking into consideration the glowing eyes too. Running into this guy without warning is most definitely not going to be a good Omen...

VALKYRIE

This ancient Norwegian warrior queen will keep warm whatever the weather thanks to her fur-lined armour. A terrifying sight in battle, her glowing eyes would strike fear into even the bravest of opponents.

P.A.N.D.A. TEAM LEADER

This skin is perfect if the way you like to play is to consume a scavenged apple, take out an opponent, and then flee the scene. Because a panda always eats, shoots, and leaves! This kind of comedy is wasted on you lot, isn't it?

SERIES SKINS

BIG CHUGGUS

This big fella is addicted to drinking slurp juice, so much so that he can't survive without it! He used to be a character in the game itself, but now you can buy him as a skin and take control of him yourself!

DARKHEART

She might look like a statue, but Darkheart is not one for sitting still! This all-action lady was part of the Dark Series, and her glowing purple eyes light the way to her next victim. Be afraid!

ASTRO JACK

This awesome skin is immediately recognisable as having the imagery made famous by Marshmello. It's pretty much impossible not to look cool when using this outfit – just concentrate on laying down covering fire rather than great tunes!

ICON SERIES | OUTFIT

ASTRO JACK

Out of this world.
Part of the **Travis Scott** set.
Introduced in **Chapter 2, Season 2**.
[*Selectable Styles*]

Ⓥ **2,000**

Ⓧ **GET V-BUCKS**

Ⓐ **PREVIEW STYLES**

Reactive Outfit: Reacts to damage!

Ⓐ [P2] TAKE CONTROL (HOLD)   Ⓡ CAMERA

HARLEY QUINN

This member of the Suicide Squad needs no introduction! Harley Quinn is a much sought after skin that doesn't come round very often so if you see her in the store and you want her – buy her while you have the chance!

REY

The last in a long line of Jedi, Rey joined the Fortnite universe during the Star Wars collaboration at the start of Chapter 2. The island seems to have stripped her of her powers though, so she needs to use weapons to eliminate her opponents instead of the Force. Shame!

THEGREFG

Yup, that's right, the YouTuber himself has his own skin in the game! If you're a fan of this Twitch star then now you can play as him yourself. Perhaps this will pave the way for more YouTubers to get their own skins – who would you most like to see added to the store?

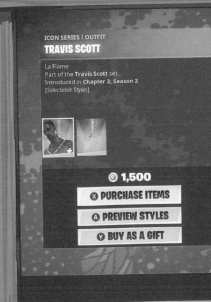

TRAVIS SCOTT

The alternative hip-hop star gave a memorable live performance in Chapter 2 Season 2, which culminated with the release of his own skin! It looks just like the man himself, even down to the tattoos (though he's added a couple since then!)

50 THINGS YOU MUST DO IN FORTNITE!

It's not all about Victory Royales and emotes, you know. There are so many different things you can do in Fortnite – here are some of our favourite ways to add **even more fun** to what is an already brilliant game. **How many of our challenges can you pull off?**

1 GET A HEADSHOT ELIMINATION WITH A SNIPER RIFLE

It might sound straightforward enough, but the sniper rifle is one of the hardest weapons to master. If you bag yourself a powerful one, perhaps a Legendary or Epic weapon, then you'll certainly have the firepower to secure a one-shot elimination if you catch someone in the head with it. Doing so, however, is a very different matter!

2 SCORE AN ELIMINATION USING A COMMON PISTOL

The common pistol may as well fire water for all the damage it does, but if you're after the ultimate burn for an opponent, knocking them out of the game using this weapon is ideal. You'll need to be quick and fire multiple shots (there's no way one shot will take them down unless they are already on their last legs from a previous battle).

3 ELIMINATE SOMEONE WHILE THEY ARE STILL GLIDING

This is a tough challenge, and relies on you hitting the ground and finding a decent weapon right from the start – ideally something decent at range such as a sniper rifle or assault rifle. Then it's a case of keeping your eyes and ears open and identifying an unfortunate opponent who has chosen to drop nearby.

4 GRAB A VICTORY ROYALE IN SOLO MODE

It's the aim of the game after all! Can you get yourself to the top of the pile in solo mode, coming out ahead of 99 rivals for the crown? To succeed, you'll need skill and a little bit of luck – and, of course, this book which gives you loads of useful hints and tips to keep you ahead of the crowd!

9 TAKE IT SLOW

Try to play an entire game while crouched. On the plus side, you'll be harder to detect while you skulk around in the shadows, but it means crossing open spaces is incredibly risky and if you're caught in a battle then you could be in big trouble. Playing this way is a great way to teach yourself how to be sneaky and stealthy because you've got no other option!

5 RUN AN OPPONENT OVER WITH A CAR

Grab yourself a car – something with a lot of speed and good handling is best. On your way through the island, keep an eye out for anyone who is not taking cover – crossing a field, for example, or pre-occupied with a gun battle. Your challenge is to drive at them at full speed, knocking them down and causing enough damage to eliminate them.

7 RIDE A FIRE HYDRANT IN THROUGH A WINDOW

In lots of the locations in Fortnite, you'll have seen fire hydrants in the street. However, you might not know that these can be used to your advantage! If you shoot the top off a fire hydrant, you can then use the resulting water jet to get yourself airbound. Using a fire hydrant in this way, try to access a building via an upstairs window!

10 CAUGHT IN A TRAP

Securing eliminations using standard weapons is pretty straightforward. Much more cunning is required, however, to secure an elimination using a trap. Try setting one immediately behind a closed door for an opponent to blunder into. You can even try and lure them in, either by making a noise so they come to investigate, or letting them see you and chase you, so you can lead them straight into your prepared trap!

6 THE THREE LITTLE PIGS CHALLENGE

Play as a trio, but with a special set of rules. One of you can only build using wood, one of you can only build using metal, and one of you can only build using stone! It will mean you need to work very closely as a trio – especially staying close to whoever is building with wood in case you need any walls putting up quickly to provide cover!

8 IS THIS THE LAST STOP?

Try playing a game where you stay on the Battle Bus until the very end – when you're kicked off! This will mean you are one of the last people to land, and you are unlikely to be too near any decent loot, adding an interesting twist.

11 THE FOUR CORNERS CHALLENGE

This is one to try in squads! Each player must land in a different corner of the map, and you then need to work your way back to each other so you can fight as a group. You'll need to be sneaky and stealthy while you're on your own, because you won't stand a chance if you run into a group of four players working as a team.

12 HAND-TO-HAND COMBAT

Securing an elimination with a weapon is one thing, but to secure an elimination with real flair, you need to do it with your harvesting tool! This is no easy task, because each hit will only cause 20HP damage to your opponent. That means five hits if they have full health, and ten if they have armour too!

13 HE SHOOTS HE SCORES!

Dotted around the island are lots of footballs and beachballs – but did you know you can kick them around? Why not try dribbling a ball from one location to another? You could even try and help your ball survive into the final storm circle! This is easier to achieve in squads, and can teach you better communication and teamwork skills too!

14 STORM ELIMINATION

Because of the colour difference, it's not always easy for a player inside the storm circle to see a player who is in the storm. Use that to your advantage, and try to eliminate another player while you are in the storm – they won't know what hit them!

15 SWAP SHOP

Instead of only picking up the good stuff, you have to drop ALL your equipment after every elimination and replace it with whatever your fallen opponent was carrying. If they only had basic weapons, or no weapons, then that's what you're stuck with! It's a great way to improve your skills with all the weapons in the game, as it stops you only using your favourites.

16 IT'S ONLY A FLESH WOUND

Any sensible Fortnite player will make sure they are carrying a couple of MedKits in case they sustain injuries, then find somewhere safe to hunker down and heal up. Try playing without giving yourself that luxury. You can use and replenish your shield, but you can't boost your health in any way. It will teach you to take extra care about building cover and not taking unnecessary risks – vital skills for any Fortnite player to master!

17 DOES ANYONE HAVE A BAND AID?

Healing team mates is an important part of any group game, especially Team Rumble – so why not make it the focus of your activities? Play as a medic – equip yourself with only MedKits, Bandage Bazookas, Shield Potions and whatever foraged goodies you can get your hands on, then focus on healing your team mates.

18 SIT TIGHT

Choose somewhere to drop and stay there, unless you are forced to move by the storm circle (in which case move to a safe named location and stay there instead). If you land at the same location a few times in a row, you'll also learn which buildings are the best ones to base yourself in, and where the best loot is likely to be – all of which can help make you a better player when you go back to moving between locations!

23 SPECIAL FORCES

Play a squads game where each player has a pre-defined specialism and must pick up weapons that support it. For example, one of you can ONLY carry a sniper rifle, while another can only carry shotguns. To make it extra tough you can even designate one player as a doctor and all they can do is carry items that will heal the rest of the team.

19 BUILD IN AN OPPONENT

This is a really tricky skill to master, but it will infuriate any opponent that you manage to do it to! The aim is to completely trap your opponent in a structure you have built by quickly building around them, including a roof. For extra flair points, you can include a trap in your construction, or simply unleash some explosive weapons on them to finish the job off!

21 FOOT SOLDIER

Try playing a whole game where you aren't allowed to set foot in a vehicle of any description. No cars, no choppers, no way to move quickly! It means you'll probably be doing a lot of legwork, but this will also teach you the importance of being aware of where the storm is, and where it's moving to.

24 I NEVER HURT ANYBODY!

One of the hardest challenges in Fortnite, and for many the holy grail of gaming – can you win a game of Fortnite without a single elimination? Naturally, averting combat is the main way to progress here, getting yourself into the final few. From there, you'll need to think laterally. Can you build an opponent into a box so that the storm finishes them? Can you use a vehicle or a pressure grenade to push an opponent into the storm so that the storm itself finishes them off? If this is your aim, remember that you can stock up with MedKits and Shield Potions galore too!

22 SPAWN ISLAND CHALLENGE

This is quite a well-known Fortnite challenge and you might have seen it on YouTube! It's a pretty straightforward scenario – you must run round the spawn island while you wait for the game to start, and collect whatever weapons you can. When the game starts, you can ONLY pick up the weapon types you found on the spawn island.

20 RAINBOW INVENTORY

There's an obvious advantage in Fortnite to picking up the best weapons available at every opportunity – but where's the challenge in that? Instead, try to secure yourself a rainbow inventory, where you carry one weapon from each class ranging from common to Legendary.

30 MULTI-ELIMINATION

You'll probably find this challenge easier to achieve if you are playing in squads or Team Rumble mode. The skill is to eliminate more than one opponent with a single weapon. The ideal way to do this is with a grenade, and you'll be most likely to pull it off if you are fighting against team-mates who are close to each other.

25 LOOTBAITING BRILLIANCE

Find a nice collection of goodies – perhaps a recently opened chest, or the dropped inventory of a fallen opponent – and hide yourself somewhere nearby. Select a powerful short range weapon and wait. Before too long, an excited player will spot the shiny toys just waiting to be picked up and bound over to collect them. That's your cue – step out from your cover and blast them!

26 FIRST MAN DOWN

Another fairly simple challenge is to make sure yours are the first boots to land on the island.
Leave the Battle Bus as soon as you can, then skydive straight down. Try to make sure your glider opens while you are over water or low land, then glide to a mountain top to minimise the time spent in the air.

28 CHESTS ARE OFF LIMITS

You're not allowed to open chests at all – you can only take weapons and provisions that you find lying around the map, or that you take from defeated opponents. This will give you far fewer options – though if you are clever, you can lootbait unopened chests and let someone else open them for you!

31 ACHIEVE THE CLEAN SWEEP

This will encourage you to become proficient in all the different game modes, challenging you to secure a Victory Royale in Solo, Duos, Trios, Squads and Team Rumble modes. That's a whole lot of winning to be done, so you'll need to be proficient in every one of those modes. Are you up to the challenge?

27 PART OF A TEAM

Why not all suit up with skins that are related to each other, sending the other squads in your game a message that you're a team and you mean business! You could all play as different Avengers, or Star Wars skins. You might all choose a sporting theme, or wear the scariest skins you can find. Alternatively, all play as default skins – people will think you're a bunch of noobs and you might be able to take them by surprise!

29 PLANNING PERMISSION REJECTED

For this Fortnite challenge, you're not allowed to build. That includes defensive walls when under fire, healing huts, the lot. You'll need to plan your route carefully too, because you won't be able to use ramps to reach high ground as you flee from the storm.

32 DROPPING THE BOOGIE BOMB

In the early days of Fortnite, it was all about the dancing. In more recent times, it's taken something of a backseat – so it's up to YOU to bring the boogie back! You have to dance after EVERY elimination – no excuses! Make sure you've picked a full range of dances so it doesn't get boring on your way to that Victory Royale!

33 CATCH IT TO USE IT

To make for a real challenge, why not only allow yourself to use weapons that you catch from fishing? You can't open chests or pick up anything you find, with the exception of fishing rods. You'll need to try and make sure you land near a body of water, and somewhere likely to be home to a fishing rod or two, then get some weaponry on board sharpish.

34 WARM YOURSELF BY THE FIRE

Lots of players forget that they can use the campfires in Fortnite to heal themselves. By allowing yourself ONLY to be healed by camp fires will really help you start to notice where they are – information that might come in handy when you're injured and don't have any healing items in your inventory.

35 COMMON AS MUCK

The lure of shiny better weapons is an ever-present temptation in Fortnite, but you can always take a disciplined approach to upgrades – by denying yourself. See if you can play through a game using only common weapons – your inventory must consist of grey weapons and no hint of colour!

36 WEAR IDENTICAL GEAR

Take the idea of being squadmates a step further by all dressing in identical gear! Mimic everything, down to styles and back bling before you head into combat. There's actually a practical advantage to this, because you can confuse other squads. Throw in a couple of decoy grenades and you have TOTAL carnage for anyone trying to hunt your squad down!

37 DUKES OF HAZZARD

This challenge requires a little bit of planning ahead – it works well as a squad, but you can pull it off playing alone. Firstly, build a huge ramp on or near a road – the higher the better! Then leap behind the wheel of a car and see just how much air you can grab! Bonus points awarded if you manage to land on any of your opponents!

38 BUSHCAMPING

Find a bush, ideally one fairly central on the map, and hide in it. You can ONLY leave your cover if the storm closes in. You must now take out as many opponents as you can from the cover of the bush. If you run low on ammo, you are allowed to nip out to pick up what they drop, but after that – straight back into your bush!

39 THE UPGRADE CHALLENGE

You can play this challenge in two different ways, depending on whether there are upgrade benches available at the time. Start with a common weapon, and upgrade it through every status until you end up with a legendary version. You can either upgrade the weapon yourself using resources and the benches, or only pick up weapons that are the next level up from the one you own.

40 FALL TO THEIR DOOM

If you encounter anyone building a tall sniping tower, then see if you can eliminate them via fall damage by destroying the bottom of the tower. Grenades are probably your best bet for this mission, or a rocket launcher. Get your timing right and they won't have time to escape or build another tower.

41 DROP IT LIKE IT'S HOT

If you're anything like us, you begin to feel a certain affinity for the weapons you pick up in game, and like to hold on to any that you've secured a few eliminations with. Let's step out of that safety zone then, shall we? Try playing the game as normal, but dropping any weapon that you secure a kill with immediately. It'll certainly keep you on your toes!

42 THE BEAR GRYLLS CHALLENGE

Around the island there are usually plenty of items to be found – whether it's fish, fruit and veg, or mushrooms. For an added challenge, try playing a game so that these items are the only way you can heal yourself. No MedKits, no Bandages, no Shield Potions. Just whatever you can find or catch for yourself. Can you find enough items to ensure your survival?

45 MOTORBOAT ROCKET ATTACK

The motorboat front-mounted rocket is great for destroying buildings, but the slow-moving nature of the missile means it's a little harder to deploy it successfully against an opponent on the ground. To do so, you'll need to be fairly close to them, which will leave you at risk of them hitting you too – so be quick, and be accurate!

48 SHHH! THEY'LL HEAR US!

Try playing through an entire game using only silenced weapons. These can be pretty scarce, so you'll need to exercise caution in the early stages of the game until you have found one. Using it will make it much harder for your opponents to find you – the trade-off is that you are unlikely to be able to do much damage at range.

43 SAY BOOM BOOM BOOM!

Try playing a whole game where the only weapons you can carry are explosive ones! Explosive traps are fair game, as are grenades, rocket launchers and anything else goes boom – but you're not allowed normal weapons!

46 HIJACK SITUATION

Hijack a boat being driven by an opponent. You'll need to be pretty close to them first, which might mean finding a hiding place near a river or lake first. Once you're in the back of the boat, you'll be able to blast the driver while they can't return fire. They'll probably try to bail though, so make sure you have a sensible weapon equipped (like a shotgun) and you're quick to pull the trigger!

49 BURN BABY BURN

Try to secure an elimination not by shooting your opponent, but by igniting the environment around them. You can achieve this in two main ways – you could use grenades to set their building alight, for example, or shoot a petrol can or an explosive cannister to cause an explosion.

44 CHOPPER BY NAME

When flying a chopper, keep an eye out for any opponents on foot down below. If you spy a potential victim, try swooping down at them and angling the chopper so that you eliminate them using the choppers blades.

47 ANYONE THERE?

Did you know you can ring the doorbells by the front doors of some houses? Working in pairs or teams, approach a building with an opponent in and ring the doorbell. While they are expecting you to come in through the front door, have your team mates launch an assault through the back door, the walls or the roof instead!

50 KEEP WHAT YOU START WITH

A big part of Fortnite is finding better weapons as you progress into the game. However, try removing the temptation to go looking for better gear by limiting yourself to the first things you pick up. In other words, you're not allowed to swap out any of the items in your inventory. You can approach this in two ways – pick up the first six items you find and make the most of it, or be selective and only pick up weapons you know you'll want to keep...